CW00321975

Safe in His Love

Illustrated by Lyn Ellis

Kevin Mayhew

First published in Great Britain in 1993 by

KEVIN MAYHEW LTD
Rattlesden
Bury St Edmunds
Suffolk   IP30 0SZ
England

LUTHERAN PUBLISHING HOUSE
205 Halifax Street
Adelaide
SA 5000
Australia

ISBN   0 86209 342 2

Printed in Hong Kong

Contents

Hold My Hand

Hold my hand, Lord.
Walk me through the loneliness
and the valley of my sorrow.
Hold onto me when I'm too afraid
to think about tomorrow.
Let me lean on you, Lord,
when I'm too weary to go on.
Hold my hand, Lord, through the night
until I see the light of dawn.

You Are There

In this long night of my faith, Lord,
sorrow seems to have no end.
Yet I know the warmth and comfort
of a never failing friend.

So I rest, securely sheltered
in your love and gentle care,
knowing even in the darkness
there is light.
For you are there.

Trust in God

I depend on God alone;
I put my hope in him.
He alone is my protector and Saviour;
he is my defender
and I shall never be defeated.
May salvation and honour depend on God:
he is my strong protector;
he is my shelter.
My people, trust in God at all times!
Tell him all your troubles,
because he is our refuge.

PSALM 62:5-8

The Lord Our Protector

I lift up my eyes to the hills.
From whence does my help come?
My help comes from the Lord,
who made heaven and earth.
He will not let your foot be moved,
he who keeps you will not slumber.
Behold, he who keeps Israel
will neither slumber nor sleep.

PSALM 121

Take Courage!

I can't change what you're going through,
I have no words to make a difference,
no answers or solutions
to make things easier for you.

But if it helps in any way
I want to say I care.
Please know that even when you're lonely
you're not alone.

I'll be here,
supporting you with all my thoughts,
cheering for you with all my strength,
praying for you with all my heart.

For whatever you need,
for as long as it takes –

Lean on my love.

Don't Quit

When things go wrong
as they sometimes will;
when the road you are trudging
seems all uphill;
when funds are low and debts are high
and you want to smile
but you have to sigh;
when care is pressing you down a bit,
rest, if you must,
but don't you quit.

Life is strange
with its twists and turns,
as every one of us sometimes learns,
and many a failure turns about
when they might have won
had they stuck it out.
Don't give up
though the pace seems slow.
You may succeed with another blow.
Success is failure turned inside out,
the silver tint of the cloud of doubt,
and you never can tell
how close you are;
it may be near when it seems so far.
So stick to the fight
when you're hardest hit.
It's when things seem worst
you must not quit.

When Dreams are Broken

When dreams are broken things
and joy has fled,
there is Jesus.
When hope is a struggle
and faith a fragile thread,
there is Jesus.

When grief is a shadow
and peace unknown,
there is Jesus.
When we need the assurance
that we're not alone,
there is Jesus.

Fresh as the Morning

Hope returns when I remember
this one thing:
the Lord's unfailing love and mercy
still continues,
fresh as the morning,
as sure as the sunrise.
The Lord is all I have,
and so I put my hope in him.
The Lord is good to everyone
who trusts in him,
so it is best for us to wait in patience,
to wait for him to save us.

LAMENTATIONS 3:21-26

13

Do Not Be Afraid

Do not be afraid,
for I have redeemed you.
I have called you by your name;
you are mine.

When you walk through the waters,
I'll be with you;
you will never sink beneath the waves.

When the fear of loneliness is looming,
then remember I am at your side.

You are mine, O my child,
I am your Father,
and I love you with a perfect love.

BASED ON ISAIAH 43: 1-5

Lord, Your Way is Perfect

Lord, your way is perfect:
help us always to trust in your goodness,
so that, walking with you
and following you in all simplicity,
we may possess quiet
and contented minds,
and may cast all our care on you,
for you care for us.
Grant this, Lord,
for your dear Son's sake,
Jesus Christ.

This is the confidence
which we have in him
that if we ask anything
according to his will
he hears us.

I JOHN 5:14

Peace I leave with you; my peace I give you.
I do not give to you as the world gives.
Do not let your hearts be troubled
and do not be afraid.

JOHN 14:27

Do not be anxious about anything,
by prayer and petition,
with thanksgiving,
present your requests to God.
And the peace of God,
which transcends all understanding,
will guard your hearts and your minds
in Christ Jesus.

PHILIPPIANS 4:7

Know that I am with you always:
yes, even to the end of time.

MATTHEW 28:20

The comforting thing about prayer
is that it reaches heaven
by whatever words the heart
chooses to express.

Lord, may we find peace in your love,
joy in your mercies
and strength in your touch.

Let us then approach
the throne of grace with confidence,
so that we may receive mercy
and find grace to help us
in our time of need.

HEBREWS 4:16

My grace is sufficient for you,
for my power is made
perfect in weakness.

2 CORINTHIANS 12:9

Loving Care

May God,
who understands each need,
who listens to every prayer,
bless you and keep you
in his loving, tender care.

My God will meet all your needs
according to his riches in Christ Jesus.

PHILIPPIANS 4:19

20

Never Alone

O Lord,
never let us think that
we can stand
by ourselves
and not need you.

He stands waiting
to share his strength with you,
to love and comfort you,
to give his peace to you.
Hope in his love.

21

I am With You

Be strong and courageous.
Do not be afraid or discouraged,
for I, the Lord your God,
am with you wherever you go.

JOSHUA 1:9

His Love

May his love enfold you.
May his peace surround you.
May his light touch you.

Together

Lord, help me remember
that nothing is going
to happen today
that you and I
cannot handle together.

Tomorrow

Don't worry
about tomorrow:
God is already there!

The Twenty-Third Psalm

The Lord is my shepherd,
I shall not want.

He makes me lie down
in green pastures.
He leads me beside still waters;
he restores my soul.

He guides me in paths
of righteousness
for his name's sake.

Even though I walk through
the valley of the
shadow of death,
I fear no evil;
for you are with me;
your rod and your staff comfort me.

You prepare a table before me
in the presence of my enemies.
You anoint my head with oil.

My cup overflows.
Surely goodness and love
shall follow me all the days of my life.
And I shall live in the house
of the Lord for ever.

I Am With You Always

In the springtime of your life,
when joy is new,
and when the summer brings
the fullness of your faith,
I'm there with you.
I am with you in the autumn
of your years,
to turn to gold every memory
of your yesterdays,
to banish winter's cold.

I am with you in the sunshine,
when your world glows warm and bright.
I am with you when life's shadows
bring long hours of endless night.
I am with you every moment,
every hour of every day.
Go in peace upon life's journey,
for I'm with you all the way.

How blest are those who
know their need for God;
the kingdom of heaven is theirs.

How blest are the sorrowful;
they shall find consolation.

How blest are those of a gentle
spirit; they shall have the
earth for possession.

How blest are those who hunger
and thirst to see right prevail;
they shall be satisfied.

How blest are those who show mercy:
mercy shall be shown to them.

How blest are those whose hearts
are pure; they shall see God.

How blest are the peacemakers;
God shall call them his sons.

How blest are those who have suffered
persecution for the cause of right;
the kingdom of heaven is theirs.

How blest are you when you suffer
insults and persecution and every
kind of calumny for my sake. Accept
it with goodness and exultation, for
you have a rich reward in heaven.

MATTHEW 5:3-12

God is the Answer

He comes as a Companion to
the lonely,
a Faithful Friend
who cares and understands.
He comes as a Physician
to the hurting,
with tenderness
and healing in his hands.

He comes as a Protector
to the helpless,
a Shepherd who calls
all his lambs by name,

a Father who sees
every child as special,
whose gentle heart
loves each of us the same.

He comes, the Consolation
of the suffering,
the Light that breaks
through darkness and despair.
He comes, and we discover
that his presence
is the loving answer to
our every prayer.

God's Promises

God has not promised
sun without rain,
joy without sorrow,
peace without pain.
But God has promised
strength for the day,
rest from the labour,
light for the way,
grace for the trials,
help from above,
unfailing sympathy,
undying love.

In Quietness

Loving God,
in your majestic quietness,
where I know nothing can grasp you,
no word define you,
no prayer bend you,
there I find my deepest security
and the purest awe.

In sorrow and suffering
go straight to God in confidence,
and you will be strengthened,
enlightened and instructed.

You Are No Stranger . . .

You are no stranger
to my heavy heart, Lord.
You take upon yourself
the grief I bear.

I find strength and hope, Lord,
in your promise
that where I am,
you also will be there.

Come to me, all who labour and are
heavy laden, and I will give you
rest. Take my yoke upon you, and
learn from me; for I am gentle and
lowly in heart, and you will find
rest for your souls. For my yoke
is easy and my burden is light.

MATTHEW 11:28-30

If the Son makes you free, you will
be free indeed.

JOHN 8:36

You Are Loved

There comes a time in life
when tears fall unheeded,
until we look up,
seeing another cross on this lonely hill.
What a dear friend we have in Jesus,
who bears all our pain in his heart,
who catches us up in his strong arms
and whispers to our hearts
'You are loved'.

When You're Lonely

When you're lonely,
I wish you love.

When you're down,
I wish you joy.

When you're troubled,
I wish you peace.

When things are complicated,
I wish you simple beauty.

When things look empty,
I wish you hope.

37

The Lord will turn
the darkness before you
into light.

ISAIAH 42:16

You are sad now, but I will see
you again, and your hearts will
be full of joy, a joy that no one
can take from you.

JOHN 16:22

38

Wings of Faith

Give us, Lord, a special faith,
unlimited and free,
a faith that isn't bound
by what we know or what we see.

A faith that trusts the sunshine
even when there is no light,
a faith that hears the morning song's
soft echo in the night.

A faith that somehow rises
past unhappiness or pain,
knowing that in every loss
your goodness will remain.

A faith that finds your steadfast love
sufficient for all things,
a faith that lifts the heart above
and gives the spirit wings.

39

Serenity

God grant me serenity
to accept the things I cannot change,
courage to change the things I can
and wisdom to know the difference.
Living one day at a time,
accepting hardship
as a pathway to peace,
taking as Jesus did,
this sinful world as it is,
not as I would have it.
Trusting that you will
make things right
if I surrender to your will
so that I may be reasonably happy
in this life and supremely happy
with you forever in the next.

Deep Peace . . .

Deep peace of the Running Wave to you.
Deep peace of the Flowing Air to you.
Deep peace of the Quiet Earth to you.
Deep peace of the Shining Stars to you.
Deep peace of the Son of Peace to you.

CELTIC BENEDICTION

41

Footprints

One night I had a dream.
I dreamed I was walking along
the beach with God,
and across the sky flashed
scenes from my life. For each scene
I noticed two sets of footprints
in the sand, one belonged to me
and the other to God.
When the last scene of my life
flashed before me I looked back at
the footprints in the sand. I noticed
that at times along the path of life
there was only one set of footprints.

I also noticed that it happened at
the very lowest and saddest times

of my life. This really bothered me
and I questioned God about it.
'God, you said that once I decided
to follow you, you would walk
with me all the way, but I noticed
that during the most troublesome
times in my life there is only one
set of footprints. I don't understand
why in times when I needed you
most, you would leave me.'
God replied, 'My precious, precious child,
I love you and I would never, never
leave you during your times of
trials and suffering.
When you see only one
set of footprints
it was then that I carried you.'

A Blessing

May the Lord bless you
and take care of you;

May the Lord be kind
and gracious to you;

May the Lord look on you with favour
and give you peace.

NUMBERS 6:22-27

44

Be at Peace

Do not look forward
to what might happen tomorrow;
the same everlasting Father
who cares for you today
will take care of you
tomorrow and every day.
Either he will shield you
from suffering
or he will give you
unfailing strength to bear it.
Be at peace, then, and put aside
all anxious thoughts and imaginings.

Why?

Wisdom is not knowing all the answers
to the problems of each day.
Not knowing why this has happened to me
and not to someone else.
Not soaking up all the knowledge
this world can offer,
but knowing that behind the whole of life,
for now and evermore, God is sovereign
and, though I may not understand,
he is working to make us

each according to his plan.
If we ask, there is an answer
to each problem,
though it may not be the one
we want to hear.
Believe your God will take
your hand if you allow.
Let him guide your every step,
and when you feel unsure
believe that he knows best.